Brand Building

Beginners Guide to Social Media and Brand Building

By: Donald Charles

Introduction

Conclusion

Introduction

Brand building is essential for today's companies. No matter if it is a big brand, or a less known, but every product has to have its customers and consumers. Also, every person who became a brand has to have a fan-base to go by the name of a brand. Today's world is dictated by the online virtual world. It became essential to dive into the world of the Internet to become known to the world. Newspapers and the TV were replaced by the online ads, blogs, articles, platforms, social media, where the common man also has a word to say. Indeed, everyone has the freedom to comment on everything. The trend or way of life affected brands as well. Brands can use it to their benefit by regarding it as a way of communication with their customers and consumers, but it also comes with the downside that people are free to criticize your every move.

This book is aimed at those who want to create and establish a brand by using online tools, social networks, and platforms. Of course, Twitter, Facebook, LinkedIn, YouTube, Google Plus, Tumblr, Instagram, and Pinterest play a crucial role in finding the target audience, presenting the brand (or yourself as a brand), establishing a customer base and a good reputation.

The quality of the brand is out of the question here, it has to be good, unique, speak to the masses, but the topic is more about how to communicate it to people, how to persuade them of the brand quality.

Another challenge relates to being different than others who are also competing for the attention of millions of Internet users.

The book focuses on a strategic approach to brand building and using online platforms to your benefit. Learn how to master your website, blog, social network profiles and YouTube channels with this unique book. It will help you to understand the essence of branding and the difference between marketing and branding.

The book reflects on many aspects of the digital era and age and what iii means in today's world to remain fresh and desirable as a brand.

Creating a brand is also associated with the unconsciousness of consumers and the emotions your brand triggers in them. Basically, that is the most important feature to maintain a brand long-term, since customer develops loyalty based on their emotions and perception.

□

Chapter 1: What Is Brand Building?

Brand building is according to many dictionaries as the systemin which a company or retail business creates or improves the customers' knowledge of the products or services and opinions of a brand. It is also explained as the process of value creation for consumers. Nike, Gucci, Dolce and Gabbana, Dior, Apple, there is no person on Earth who has not heard about these brands and companies. All of these are well-established brands, which made their presence known to the entire world.

All of these brands (except Apple which is part of the high-tech revolution) created a long-lasting reputation before the Internet revolution and the many social media which are now regularly used for marketing and advertising.

The social media also became brands for themselves and made a name in technology. Facebook, Twitter, Instagram are also brands which are used for marketing other brands or brands-to-be.

If you are a small-business owner or have an idea for a business, you probably have thought of letting people know via social media to draw attention to your product or services.

Brands are closely connected to the perception of the consumers. The perception is based on the experience the consumers who try out a specific product/service and form an opinion.

There are three major types of brands:

1.   Product brand is built on the experience consumers gain with a specific product, i.e. a car, food, etc.

2.   Service brand is established on the experience costumers have with a specific service offered and delivered

3.   Retail brand is built of the combined experience including both, of product and service.

Chapter 2: Benefits Of Building A Captivating Brand

With a brand, you can gain major benefits wherever you go. Brand building is associated with creating an image of the company which consumers will relate to. It is important to develop the association between positive attributes and your brand at the subconscious level. The ultimate goal is to reach consumers on an emotional level. Once the brand gains recognition and becomes widely known, the brand will be one step ahead of competitors.

With an established brand, you are able to set the prices as high as you want and you will not lose customers. Also, every new product you launch into the market will be accepted very fast. When people see a branded product and a one that is not, they will probably opt for the branded more expensive one.

Recognition means to have a logo which will be unique and immediately associated with you. The bitten apple of Apple will always be associated with the brand and Steve Jobs. You have to give the brand a personality which is distinctive form other products. It should indicate your relationship to customers and clients.

As we said, you are able to set your own prices without any compromises, and a brand will actually hit sales records. A high-quality trusted brand will yield higher sales. If a customer likes a specific brand, they will be probably willing to try other products by the same manufacturer.

It is important to become aware of the psychological aspects of a brand. It is known as brand experience and means that the customers develop a relationship with the brand. It is the way the brand is perceived by the customer and user. It also refers to what people think of when they see your logo and what emotions are evoked. It is important for a brand to set itself apart from other products, by proving to people that their brand is indeed different and worth the money.

Brands can protect you from price undercutting even during times of economic changes. Weak brands usually have to compete with the rival companies to offer a better price (i.e. cheaper) and are often affected by poor economies. Strong brands know their value, and they know that consumers know their value, they compete to offer quality and the best service, not price.

People tend to think that spending more money for a branded item is worth it. They have no problems to save a larger sum to afford a product from a trusted brand.

Your employees will also work tighter together because they are driven by the same idea and same beliefs. You will have a strong team behind you which pushes your ideas through. It is not a secret that brands employ people who truly believe in the brand, which is more important than qualifications to brand makers.

There are different strategies to test the brand's strengths whereby the brand's positive and negative sides are being assessed and compared to competitors' products. The process is called brand management which means that the focus is truly set on the brand development. The brand management will always try to find new ways to improve certain brand aspects to make it more appealing to the wider public.

There is a difference between marketing and branding. Marketing is more related to temporary results, while branding generates long-term success. Therefore, be aware of the difference, and your goal is always a continuous success.

Tactical short-term marketing strategies involve the presentation of the product, marketing campaigns, events, etc., while branding means to get into the heads and hearts of customers which will later pay off.

☐

Chapter 3: How To Create A Brand

There are several steps in brand creation. Everyone create a brand who has a great business idea and original marketing tricks and strategies. Today's Internet world made marketing even cheaper and does not cost thousands of dollars like setting up billboards or making a TV commercial to communicate it to the public. The Internet is really a miraculous invention, enabling the most distant and isolated countries to get a hold of a product marketed on the other side of the world. To create and develop a brand, one should be first of all define a brand.

You have to identify your brand, what it stands for and what its purpose is. A good beginning would be to make a list of all the essential strengths and values your brand brings to the table. Think carefully in order not to miss something. Your brand should in some way reflect your qualities and skills. You also have to take into account what is in for the consumers. Nowadays, a brand has to reflect economic, environmental and social standards to contribute to the well-being of customers and the environment.

The other step is to think of what makes your brand different from the competition's. There are thousands of the same products, but your product has to offer a special feature or quality, or evoke a different kind of experience or feeling in the consumers. Uniqueness and originality are the keys that open the hearts of consumers. Also, the brand has to offer something that is of general use, a must-have kind of product or service.

Even if a product is not needed in everyday life, strong marketing strategies can make customers feel as if the product is a must-have and they will not resist to buy it. Still, if you want a long-term brand, your brand will be a product or service which makes life easier and better than the rivalry companies.

After you thought of the special value only your brand offers, use the most effective marketing strategies to draw attention to your product/service and the value it brings, only offered by you, and no one else. Make consumers appreciate your value and see the difference between yours and the other's product.

Building a brand is not a once-in-a-lifetime event. It is rather a-whole- lifetime event which requires nurture, care, preservation and maintenance. It takes time and continuous work. You will have to expose your brand, at sometimes even reinvent yourself, reinforce the brand's values, etc. you have to assume other roles which will help you get more exposure. Now, we come to the social media communication channels which can help you in keeping customers in the loop with the development of your brand, any changes, sales announcements, reinvention techniques, etc.

You cannot create a brand independent form yourself. A brand goes and is supposed to be in line with your personality and image. What people think, say and know about you, i.e. their perception of you will be automatically linked and transferred to the brand. The strategies you employ should be consistent in order to develop a recognizable pattern which automatically associates people with your brand.

As we said, your brand cannot be separated from you but is also needs an individual personality. Develop your brand's personality by giving it the features consumers perceive as admirable, with which they can easily identify. The emotional link is inevitable here. You have to give your brands the necessary identity which will trigger emotional addiction. Just think about how tied to your phone you are, your laptop, etc.

Once you established a brand identity, you can shift yet to another trick. Freely invite consumers to participate in the brand creation. Let them know you are interested in their ideas and needs. Top brands are accustomed to creating personalized custom-made products/services on the basis of their customers' preferences. Your customers are your most important link, and you should trust them enough to make them participate in deciding the direction of the brand. The market is already usually based on the needs of the consumers, and you should seize the opportunity to find out first-hand what your target customers would like to see in your brand or make a change, etc. this is also important for your relationship with your customer-base who will feel appreciated and important to you.

As we said creating a brand does not refer to a one-time wonder, the brand will develop through time and go through different phases ranging from silent to turbulent. To resist the pressure of time, you will probably face having to reinvent or introduce changes to the brand, etc. it will go strong at times, then again be passive, etc.

Challenges can be turned into opportunities and vice versa. With time, you will have to deal with different circumstances and turn them to your benefit by trying to enhance the values of your brand. You see that building a brand is not everything; even a bigger focus is on the follow-up activities which basically define your career.

The more successful you get, the bigger the pressure will be. You will have to justify and top the achievement before that. In order to stay on top of the things, the best would be to keep track of the band activities by checking brand awareness and engagement levels. Being involved will open new opportunities, or at least will open the door for you to think of new ideas.

Still, you have to stay true to your brand name and image, and you will always be working on the same foundations.

To sum up, it is important to build a brand, make it different and unique, give it wings and create enough wind for it to fly.

☐

Chapter 4: Eight Strategies

1.   The first thing you need to understand when creating a brand is that you are the biggest fan and advocate of your brand. You have to convey the message to the wider public; you have to have all the answers and defence tactics in case of attack by malicious tongues. Steve Jobs is the biggest ambassador of Apple and promoted his "baby" every time he could.

2.   Prepare investor for the brand. Investors have to be familiar with every step you take, and you should regularly report to them. Make them fit to understand the brand, its value, and benefits. Share with hem the obstacles you stumble upon, your worries and progress, either in an eye to eye meeting, but a video will also make it in today's dynamic world. You only have to be honest, which is sometimes easier over a video message but still, they need to know where you are at.

3.   Content marketing is also one of the most useful strategies you could use. At the end of the day, it all revolves around the content which is associated with

quality and trustworthiness of the brand. Video marketing is perfect because they allow you to be educational, fun, and inspirational. You directly address your audience, and they will automatically feel closer to you and moreover, trust you. Videos give you enough space to prove the quality of your product/service or to convince people of it. Marketing should be more about the consumers and clients, so the focus should stay on how it benefits them, rather than on sales.

4. Partner Up! Do not hesitate to associate your brand with an already renowned brand. In fact, try to set up cooperation with a prestigious brand in the same business. This will boost your own brand name and help you set up a client-base. Your business partner will promote you, and that is the best marketing. You will be accepted and perceived by your clients as one of the big players. Collaboration on such a high level should be definitely part of your plan even if you are not yet ripe enough to it at the moment.

5. Offer the best to work for the best! Many brands made a name and achieved celebrity status by not one client but THE client. Be on the lookout for big fish which have a lot of admirers, fans and followers. In that way, your business

will develop on its own and your brand will be famous before you know it. High-profile clients can definitely open numerous success doors to you. What could be useful in such a position is to secure approval to do a case study which can help you in the future. The case study includes how your contribution helped the brand or the individual, and how clients enjoyed cooperating with you.

6.   You do not need PR if you have enough fans. They can be your spokespeople, and probably they will do the job more efficiently than any paid help. The trick is their honesty. They will promote you because they believe in you. And that is the best reward and promotion you can get. Testimonials have conquered the Internet, and you should also always ask for feedback. Still, live video testimonials would enhance credibility and trust. If you could get your customers to make a video feedback on your branded product or service, that would be perfect.

7.   Brand Development will probably be necessary through time. Time brings many changes, and all of us have to adapt to these changes and new trends, new generations, etc. you will have to reach out to new techniques to promote, attract and get into the middle of things. Some conventional businesses which emerged before Internet

revolution had to jump on the revolutionary web train not to disappear from the surface.

An example can be taken on all the stars, whether actors or musicians who were stars before the digital era but they realized that they would be socially dead if they would not keep their Twitter, Instagram, Google+, Facebook, etc. you need to know where your audience is and follow them.

Sometimes it is important to assess which social networks fits your needs best. For example, wedding designers should certainly be registered on Pinterest, because 70% of Pinterest users are women from 18-34. This means that you can find your target audience at one place.

8.   Charity! If you already have a successful brand or you are on the right path, remember to give back to society. Build relationships with people on a human level as well, not only on the business level. Donate to charity, become a philanthropist, etc. of course, you should not only do it to polish your brand image, but it will help your business as well. Identify your brand with giving back and sharing and generosity. People will appreciate it, and the word will spread around.

These strategies can help you in establishing your brand in the right way. Each step is important because, nowadays, a brand cannot be separated from the personal image. You have to be the all-around favorite person to stay the darling of your industry and your fans.

Chapter 5 : How Technology Has Changed Brand Building

Today's world absolutely requires presence in the viral world. Famous people, just like brands, would be considered socially dead if they would not constantly be in touch with the public over social media. Therefore, to create a brand, it is vital to be present and represented on all platforms and networks which exist.

Even the biggest brands adapted to the digital world and entered the digital era with style. Moreover, they took it as a benefit to further present their products and advertisements.

Of course, the digital world made it harder regarding competitiveness and many products are advertised on a daily basis. So, it is also essential to make a brand which will catch the eye of the masses of Internet users. Most of the Internet ads are being ignored because they pop out all the time, and users choose not to notice them most of the time.

Think through how you want to advertise your product on the many platforms, Facebook, Twitter, Pinterest, Tumblr, Google+, YouTube, etc.

The digital age also made it possible for users to comment on the products and share their opinions with millions of other users. This can also influence the decision of buyers whether to buy or not to buy a product.

The digital age made marketing cheaper or free in contrast to the once famous TV ads which cost a fortune. The benefit is also that you can gain brand advocates, your customers become a kind of your sales managers by spreading the word.

What stays the same in the digital age is that branding is more about than just the product. It includes so many factors form your behavior, treatment of your employees to your social engagement. Branding is an overall industry.

The digital era is all about clicks, likes, comments, followers, etc. It really requires an all-around presence among the community. Also, over the Internet, people gained the feeling that brands are closer to them, that they know more about the brand and that it is more accessible.

As we see, the digital age can help you market your product for free, but it also has to overcome the obstacles of being ignored by users and trashed in the comments. Make sure to present your product to the target audience which could become potential buyers. Branding is a long-term process, and you will have to be patient, consistent, hard-headed to get your brand where you want it. Use the digital world to your advantage, in the end; is serves as a way of communication, so communicate your brand to the people.

Chapter 6: How To Reinvent Your Business Image In The Digital Age

Many companies, celebrities, and brands which became famous way before technological advancements, had to reinvent themselves as brands in the digital era. Imagine a Meryl Streep setting up her Twitter account for the first time, but yet she did. She shows loyalty to her fans, and as every professional star, she seized the opportunity of the new age to stay in touch with her fans. If people of Mary Streep caliber could dive into the digital world and keep themselves afloat, then you should be able as well.

What does it mean to reinvent yourself in the online digital world at all? It means that you should never get old, you have to entertain your consumers and cheer them up with special effects (or special offers) from time to time. The digital world is incredibly fast and has a dynamic on its own. We being only humans, have to chase after the latest technology trends. Every day something new is on the market regarding the life-changing Internet platforms.

To maintain a brand, you have to keep an updated website, which means that you should change the design from time to time, the layout, and update important and new information for your loyal customers. If you have a good branding strategy, do not push it with the changes, but apply them moderately.

We all know these brands that downgraded themselves by trying too hard to stand out. You might want to avoid that. Be loyal to your idea, just add some spice from time to time. Do not completely change your brand and style, rather upgrade it.

The digital age dictates contact with consumers now, so make sure to show up regularly on the social networks to see people's impressions and critics. Sometimes it is good to see what they have to say; maybe they can help you improve your brand with a new idea.

Chapter 7: Social Media: Facebook/Instagram/Twitter

The Internet was already a revolution for itself, but yet, the Facebook, Twitter, and Instagram revolutions were all the little big revolutions which sprang out as a result. Since the social media turned the lives of the digital generation upside down, by making it unimaginable not to login into all of the social media at least once a day. Given the attention and multiple daily visits of over 1.6 billion people on Facebook, and 400 million on Instagram, it is only natural that Facebook and Instagram became tools for business ideas and brand creation.

By advertising something on Facebook, you can get the attention of the average man, and make several thousand-people aware of your product or service within a very short period.

What is important to know is how to advertise it to make sure that the right people see it. Of course, first, you need to identify your target audience and potential product or service users. You have to advertise for the people who matter to your business. To leave a significant impression use visual aids like videos and photos. Visualization makes everything more believable and suggests trust into the specific product/service.

The first thing is to set up a page on Facebook. This will help you to connect with your target audience, and you can run your campaigns on Instagram, Facebook, and other social networks. As we said, visualization and presentation are essential. Learn how to make a captivating video which will touch the masses. Facebook provides measurement tools which will inform you on the progress and how many people joined or responded to your ads, how many visits you had, etc.

There are masses of people who started running business just over Facebook. Have you seen all the people who sell clothes on Facebook? Afterward, they open real stores with an actual physical location. Facebook can also serve to self-assess your success potential. Just as the clothes sellers who tried their luck over Facebook, and established a customer-base, they were encouraged to officially enter a business. Also, jewellery makers seem to have benefited from today's Internet Age.

There is a chain of values which define brand establishment. The chain starts with awareness, continues with consideration (on the part of the consumer), purchase, preference, and finally, loyalty. These are the phases every brand needs to go through to become a reputable brand. The first three phases can be facilitated through marketing, while the last two are rather defined by the product/service quality and attachment to the brand.

Before the Internet onrush, the TV commercials were the major source of advertising. That might have been more expensive, but it was easier to draw attention to products. Making and airing a TV commercial was associated with successful people. Nowadays, the Internet is somewhat less trusted because everyone has access to it, but with the right brand, the mistrust can be overcome. The initial chain of brand creation works differently in the world of social media. Namely, people first hear or learn about a brand, then they research it on social media and the Internet, after which, they consult their friends, and finally decide to buy it. After the purchase, they expect to have a certain interaction with the brand.

The social media environment works on different principles than pre-digital marketing strategies. Let us see what the best way is to create a brand via social media.

Articulation of your product or service is the first step. Find a catchy phrase which will draw the attention and connect to the target audience; it can be something inspirational, emotional, witty, etc. It has just to be built around your brand. To connect with the target audience or consumers, Facebook is the optimal choice. There they can participate, ask questions about the brand, etc.

Engagement of consumers is one of your targets. To get them to talk about the brand and refer further, you can use some Facebook tools to help you out. For example, different Facebook apps are focused on brand promotion as well as the Sponsored Stories ads which help promote brands. It basically turns the activities of the friends to promoted material. Sponsored Stories are associated to the Newsfeed. Company owners can use some activities of the users and feature them in the newsfeed. Usually, these activities are check-ins or any other forms of mentioning or tagging the product/service, name, etc. companies can also pay to have all check-ins featured to the Sponsored Stories section. They do not control the published information, feedbacks or check-ins, they simply gather them across Facebook and put them in the said section.

You have to exhibit a certain influence over the social media users and get close to them by maybe incorporating something that is close to them. Make sure to think of the interests of your target audience and deliver an ad which directly concerns them, their origin, habits, etc.

Reinvention and refreshing of your product/service is a key part of keeping your brand and business alive. As a businessman, understand the importance of staying relevant to customers and in the given market. You have to keep your website or Facebook page updated, tell the fans what is new with the brand, share relevant information, and sometimes even, reflect on other big events, like some big news and make them known on your site. You want to show your clients that you are close to everyday events and that you want to share with them all relevant stuff.

Chapter 8: YouTube

YouTube has its 10th anniversary this year and is also a brand for itself. Internet gave way to yet another way of expression to all the users and Internet lovers. YouTube is full of videos on all imaginable and unimaginable topics. From funny videos to educational, it encompasses every genre.

Many people got famous over YouTube by keeping and maintaining regular YouTube channels broadcasting themselves. It went that far that YouTube personality became a legit word in defining the direction of the career in entertainment. Many people are known today as YouTube personalities and created a brand out of themselves.

Usually, these personalities are strongly involved in hair and make-up products and give regular advice on how to put make-up on, how to do a specific hair style, etc. Also, some others gained popularity by giving advice and tips on dating, boys, girls, and other topics, etc. YouTube replaced TV to a certain extent, and what news anchors were before, nowadays they are YouTube channel hosts.

A good marketing strategy or a good idea is also of utmost important. One of the best examples of a YouTube awareness raising campaigns was the Ice Bucket Challenge which developed into a contagious campaign where everyone participated, from the President of the United States to your next-door neighbor. It was made for everyone who wanted to raise awareness of others and donate to a charity cause. The idea of doing the act of pouring ice-cold water (preferably with ice) over oneself and thereby challenging several more people you know to do the same, provoked mass attention. The campaign raised incredible 115 million for ALS. Many famous people helped the cause by doing the Ice Bucket Challenge themselves, and inspiring masses of people to do the same. It was a real adventure in 2014.

This campaign showed how a marketing strategy can reflect and strongly influence people, and how it is promoted and passed on from one to the other in record time. Also, it shows the power of YouTube which makes it possible to document oneself in action. Millions and millions of views account for fame nowadays.

Today, fame is also based on the number of YouTube views, Facebook page likes, Tweet likes, Twitter followers, etc. All of the popstars use it to be close to their fans and to let them know what they are up to, what they think, etc.

Many companies and stars have their own social networks management who uploads what needs to be uploaded, and promotes what needs to be promoted.

To build a brand you can use YouTube to make a great impression and to intrigue people by your offer. Make sure to have an original idea which speaks to the target audience.

Today's usual course of events is defined not by what people accidently see on the TV, but they choose what they want to watch. Mostly they stumble upon it randomly, or hear from friends and acquaintances about the great new product or YouTube clip and search for it to check it out.

There are numerous websites that are suitable for brand creation, but only some of them will make you popular. As we mentioned above, Facebook, Twitter, and LinkedIn are some of those websites. Still, what is it that sets YouTube apart, the biggest video sharing network of all times.

YouTube has a certain reputation due to the famous people who use it. It does not only include pop stars and entertainment, but universities also use it to share lectures with their students, politicians use it to make certain public announcements. The power of YouTube is related to visualization. We have already mentioned that people are more likely to respond to videos and visible contents. The video gives the opportunity to connect with the audience and viewers who will feel at one point as if they have already met you.

Videos make it possible to hear someones voice, see what they look like, their gesticulation, etc. therefore, video are the most powerful tool in making and promoting a brand in today's world. Here are some tips for all those who would like to brand their product, service, or themselves.

Consistent profile and Channel name

If you already have a brand name which you use on other websites, make sure to broadcast on YouTube under the same name, because that is what a brand is about. Be consistent! If you are in the phase of thinking of one, make sure to come up with the one you really like because you cannot change the channel name later on.

You can either go under your full real name or the name of your company, as well as under a show name for the channel. Channels featuring several faces should go under a branded company name or a topic, while channels involving only one person can be named after the individual (e.g. learn how to sky-dive with Harry Miller).

Setting up of profile

You will be required to fill out the profile data, which is good because it enables people to locate you on YouTube among millions of people who are also competing for views and attention. Upload a professional picture, your avatar, most preferably the one you use on other websites. You may also select the screenshot from your last video you automatically receive. You will get your own URL for the website representing you as a brand (e.g. bloggers).

There are different types of YouTube accounts which can be chosen. The majority of people is unaware of that. Study the different account types to see what each type offers. For example, the Guru account (recommended to experts) enables using a custom logo and attaching links.

Once you set up your YouTube channel, you have options to customize its features which will enhance the streaming of your videos when fans are watching. The "Switch to player mode" option will display your channel in the latest layout, featuring your other videos on the right side.

Key words and tags are also important to enter because on that principle your video will pop out when viewers are looking for something specific or similar. The option "Edit channel" is the option you use to enter your channel name and keywords or tags which should be related to your video's content. The tags will make it easier for people to find your video when searching through the Internet.

We are still on the topic of settings and options. You should also be aware that you can change themes and clours and set even your own picture as a background. Free YouTube designs can also be found on the Internet, so browse through the different websites to see the offers.

What you will certainly need especially when promoting brands is a solid video equipment. You can find webcams for around $100 which enable video chat. Companies should use extra equipment to look professional, like lighting, sound system and other tools which make it look like a professional TV show or TV commercial.

After the technical part, let us move to the essence of the video which is key. Your content has to be interesting and speak to masses of people. The best shot is a funny or an extremely interesting and useful video.

The advantage of making YouTube videos is that you can simply delete the video if you do not like it and do it all over again. You do not have to feel pressured because you control what is going to be broadcasted.

Try not to deviate from the theme of your channel, and all of your videos should be about the specific theme. Make sure to have a title, relevant tags, and video description. Also, attach the link of your website to promote yourself or your product/service in case people do not know your website but would like to see more.

After you have made several videos, it is time for promotion. The videos can be easily linked to Facebook and shared on your personal profile or fan page. Facebook will attract more viewers.

You can also use the option of auto-sharing to Facebook, Google Reader, Twitter. Still, you should pay attention who your target audience is. If you are promoting your business, you should share among the business community.

You can also share the YouTube video to your blog (as you probably figured out, keeping a blog is also very important in online branding). By adding your blog, you can easily repost ion your blog with few clicks.

The nature of the Internet and web search is simple; the more links you have to your video, the higher it will rank. And the natural course of events is that more people will pay attention and watch your video which contributes to your brand creation.

The traffick on YouTube is unbelievable, and it represents one of te best ways for promotion. Moreover, you decide on the content, and how you will present it to the wider public.

What YouTube Professionals Say

One has to be clear, to upload a video is not the whole job. it looks easy on the surface, but when someone uses it as a marketing tool, then, a lot of maintenance is required. YouTube professionals who managed to brand themselves and who maintain a loyal audience, give the following tips. YouTube is designed to show more and more. With every video, you open, another several pop out as suggestions. Since it works on the principle of similar content, it will simultaneously feature your content and your competitor's. Professional YouTubers say that the content is basically encircled by a lot of distractions; like ads popping out, other videos featured on the right, and the comment section. Only a small part (central part) of the platform is reserved for your content. In addition to content, broadcasters have to pay attention to how the video is perceived by viewers and what they will see.

The other tough part of YouTube is the comment section, which can be very cruel. All of the people have the right to say whatever they want and announce it publicly under the veil of anonymity. Their comments can shift the focus from the contents and make it about something else. To cope with his part, one has to know what they stand for and be confident.

Professional YouTubers also say that sometimes it simply won't work and that people will sometimes reject your content.

Sometimes it is important to use the comment section as a constructive critique. You can use it to your advantage because you will know what people would like to see from you and what is exactly they liked or did not like in the video. This applies to normal comments and excludes negative and hateful comments which are more a reflection of the commentator than your product or yourself.

As a broadcaster, it is important to assess your audience properly and if the experience you offer befits them. You have to be fully aware of what kind of message your content is supposed to convey and how it benefits your audience.

It can even happen that your content and brand are good but not right for YouTube. Maybe it is just that another medium would be far better for promotion.

The professional YouTubers love that YouTube is free and that it is creativity-friendly. No one is controlling your work or sets deadlines; you organize your own work at desired pace. Still, self-discipline does not work for all people, especially the types who tend to neglect the work unless they are made to do it. YouTube sometimes requires a lot of creativity, and it is not always possible to master creativity at such a high level, therefore, assess your product/service/yourself and think if YouTube will produce the desired outcomes.

Some of the YouTube professionals swear on collaboration. They think that it is important to cooperate and do business with people who do similar or same things as you. Thereby they can promote themselves over other channels. They push each other further and enable an overlap of the audience, and both will gain new viewers. Cooperation is viable to keep the brand in motion and alive.

Use ads to your benefit

Ads are an integral part of YouTube, and they have an impact on the viewers. They can help you foster your brand. And yet again, we have to reflect back on deciding on the target audience, would you rather focus on viewers from a specific location, or on topics people browse for.

After you decided on the target audience, there are several ways to advertise on YouTube.

One kind of ads is video player ads which appear before a video begins. They can usually be skipped in several seconds, and they have to make an impression on the viewer in the few seconds. Other ads in include non-skippable ads, ads appearing on the screen, etc.

Chapter 9: LinkedIn

LinkedIn is the most professional network of all. It was designed for business and networking on a professional level. LinkedIn has definitely the potential to boost your career, your brand and you as a professional. Over 43 million professionals are registered with LinkedIn in more than 200 countries. The professional network is very large and enables business deals on a global level. Freelancers are especially fond of LinkedIn where they can secure clients like big corporations.

LinkedIn stands as a resume statement, including references, cover letter, CV, and contact database. To establish a brand on LinkedIn, you have to take into consideration several steps.

The first one is to brand a flawless profile on LinkedIn. LinkedIn gives the freedom to cooperate to judge every individual in order to see if the particular individual fits the needs of the company. Pay attention to how you are forming your sentences (errors are a no go from the start), do not omit any details or experiences. Sometimes it helps to think about it as if you are sending a resume to your dream company and you double-check every sentence you have written. The site is professional, and you should keep up with the standard.

Your URL is important here and should read as http://linkedin.com/in/fullname. This will rank you higher in Google searches, and you will be easier to find. This option is found on your profile first under "edit," and then under "public profile URL." There, enter your full name with no space and save the changes.

The last job you listed will automatically be listed as the headline. Of course, you can change that manually. Use the headline to promote your brand if that is not the last listed.

If looking for a desired job over LinkedIn, your headline should include the desired job, not the one you have. Maybe you can rephrase it to include both.

The summary should include a brief statement about your previous experiences and the career goals you aspire to. In brand creation, you can say something about yourself and the brand of course.

The section Experience should be filled out in detail. People usually tend to list few last jobs they had. You can list all jobs you did especially those relevant for the kind of job you want to get. Consult your CV not to forget something that could be important.

LinkedIn is also known as the talent search browser, and keywords play an important role in appearing in searches. Choose the right keywords which are related to your headline and your occupation or business and dispose them on your profile.

If you are someone who has already a blog, apply over a block link. In that way, you can share your thought, emotions, standpoints, and feelings with people. You can also integrate presentations which can be made available to employers for download.

Make sure to list all your web page and blog links in the website section. In that way, the link will be associated with your URL.

The recommendation section should also be filled, even if they are always trusted. Most people are aware that the recommendations come form the group of your supporters like friends, colleagues, family members, etc. still, it is important because of the "thumbs up" icon. The number of recommendations is shown, and still, in the business world, they mean a lot. People with more recommendations definitely have better shots and are considered more reliable. You might secure recommendations from employers and list them. Some people have recommendations from celebrities, and those recommendations are very powerful.

After you set up your profile, you should aim at developing your network. It is about listing first, second and third degree contacts. The development takes a natural course; the more first-degree contacts you have, the more second and third-degree contacts will you secure. All of these contacts are relevant for connecting with people and possibly business partners or employers.

A facilitating circumstance is that LinkedIn allows contact import. You actually can transfer your contact lists from your e-mail accounts. You may also search for them individually, but that might be a little bit exhausting.

Networking is the major factor of LinkedIn. This means that you should be available, accept new contracts that add you, engage in business conversations, etc. all of that can lead you to great business opportunities and manifest your brand in a larger community.

One more trick to gather contacts is to make your e-mail visible, make it public. You can also use your URL and put it wherever you can. This includes presentations, resumes, along with e-mail, your business card, etc. Basically, promote it to draw attention.

When updating a status, you have to be aware that LinkedIn requires a more professional approach than Facebook and Twitter. You are not sharing your thoughts with your friends on Facebook, or discuss an issue with your followers on Twitter, but you actually share a business idea or something related to your brand. Check your spelling, grammar, content, style, and semantics.

LinkedIn offers numerous possibilities to get more followers and contacts, great job opportunities, etc.

One way is to start a LinkedIn group which can foster your brand. Think of a topic related to your brand and idea you want to promote and gather people around that topic. Be the initiator and leader. Some groups gain thousands of followers, and that really is a statement. Come up with a witty idea which connects you to people who share the same interests, ideas, and jobs.

It is your free choice what the group will be about and what kind of followers you want to attract, it can range form local to international. Also, invite all people who could be interested in such a topic or group. You might also promote the group on other social networks like Facebook, your blog, Twitter to draw attention to potential fans and group members. Member activity is vital for the survival of the group. But also, as soon as you share something in the group you will notice members actively taking part in it. They will also share their ideas, thoughts, etc.

You can also start an event on LinkedIn. Many people use it to arrange conferences and gather business people together. This can also serve as an excellent basis to promote your brand or any news related to your brand.

Ask and answer section can also contribute to your online presence and development. When you see a question from someone in your network, and you happen to know the answer, you should definitely help out and join the conversation. You can develop an image of a knowledgeable person who is the person to go to when in doubt.

As we already talked about brand consistency make sure to have the same avatar wherever you appear to be easier to identify and associate with your own brand. Provide also your full name and branding expression/statement.

You will have to devote some time to your LinkedIn profile and always bear in mind that LinkedIn is flooded with people who are looking for other people for business-related matters. LinkedIn can help you find the right people who can help you to establish your brand more effectively.

Chapter 10: Local SEO Attracts New Customers

Local SEO refers to the local Search Engine Optimization. It is a very powerful means to reach local customers. Local SEO use browsers like Google and Yelp to get in touch or to find business in their local areas. Be aware that your neighborhood is your friends and that everything starts with the local community. If you are good enough for them, you will be good enough to others too. Local SEO has several benefits, and it can be even called targeted marketing. When you have an ad in the newspapers, it might or might not be seen by people, but with SEO, people will actually look for you intentionally. Local SEO helps you connect with customers at the moment they need your product or service. This also promotes your business, they can and probably will recommend your brand further if satisfied with the performance of the product or service.

The Internet became popular in local communities and them also slowly and gradually shift to find what they need to the Internet. Logically, the first thing they do is to look for good services or products nearby. In the meanwhile, 58% is the number of searches for local businesses. Local services and products became a real trend, and it seems that everyone is starting out there. Appreciate your community because they can be your first step in creating your brand. Since the Internet is nothing new on the cell phones anymore, many customers use their mobile apps to find businesses around them. SEO cover mobile Internet as well, which means it increases your chances of being found.

Local SEO is really cost-effective and efficient at the same time. You will be linked to customers when they need you, which means that they are not thinking or rethinking if they want to buy what you offer, but they had made that decision already.

By now, only 10% of businesses list their location, so be one of the pioneers and surpass your competitors with his smart and simple move.

Newspaper ads are not as efficient as before. That is the sad reality (sad for the pre-Internet generations). The Internet became the major means of communication for pleasure and business. Another benefit is that 70% of clients trust reviews from the Internet. Try to get online reviews and testimonials from your clients which will attract other clients who will stand in line to get to your service or product.

It does not matter what kind of business you are running or trying to establish, all of the businesses are worth siding with SEO. Plumbers, electricians, accountants, lawyers, all professions you can think of have turned to SEO to be easier found. Actually, it becomes common practice and a regular thing that is only natural to do.

The local SEO can really advertise you in the right way and make you one of the favorite service providers or product providers in your neighborhood, block, town, district, etc. Start with your brand by ensuring the trust of your local community first. They will definitely provide a springboard for you to develop further. They will be the first step on the leather of success. Once you earn a good reputation in your own community, it will be so much easier to expand to other communities, given your acquired experience and the good word everybody puts in for you.

Some people or business people think that they do not have to show a lot of effort among their community members, and they are constantly waiting for their break-through to show their real potential. This is something that definitely raises eyebrows, not only mine but the majority's as well. First, when behaving like this, people expose themselves to the risk to never get a chance for a break-through. Second, you should even try harder when you provide a service or product for your community. at the end, neighborly solidarity should push you to make a harder effort. Your community will appreciate it and kindly cheer for you to expand your incredible services/products.

Chapter 11: The Impact of SEO in Your Branding Efforts

Building a brand has been an essential part of business for years even before the internet came into existence. With the advent of the internet and search engines, the process of building a brand has undergone a lot of changes, but it still retains its importance. With the rise of search engines, SEO came to the fore, and this became an essential part of brand building. You have already seen the relationship between local SEO and branding. However, local SEO is just one part of SEO. There is still a lot about the associations between SEO and branding that you need to know, and this chapter will explore those links.

Why SEO and Brand Building Are Linked

You see, customer perception can be important for SEO. At the same time, the image you create around your business can affect the rank of the site on Google. Why is this case?

Well, brand building is a lot like SEO as it involves a wide range of areas. Those areas also fall under the other classifications of marketing. The advantages of creating a brand are easily noticeable in the case of bigger organizations. In such cases, an image can help in leading the press stories, the online conversations around the brand and the mentions on social media.

These days, the algorithms employed by search engines are quite powerful. They are quite effective when it comes to the detection of brand mentions over the internet. Now, it is difficult for any business to ensure high-quality natural links to their website. As a result, brand mentions are certain to become a major factor for search ranking with the passage of time.

On the other hand, this is by no means the only correlation that exists between the two. The brand strategy is capable of being a direct influence to the SEO targeting strategy dependent on the brand proposition and target audience. Moreover, SEO involves the improvement of conversions, user journey, and site usability. As a result, SEO and branding have quite a few major aspects in common.

Brand Strategy and SEO

When you are creating marketing strategies, you will really need to know whom your brand is targeting if you want your

SEO to be effective. If the target audience is not considered in the strategy, the strategy is certainly flawed. After all, a brand is going to resonate with a specific audience, and it is this audience that needs to be targeted. To develop a strong brand, you require a presence and an image which can connect specifically with that audience. At the same time, the SEO campaign should aim to develop the brand image at the right level.

You need to know where your target audience spends its time online. Otherwise, it will become impossible for you to get relevant links. You will not be able to interact with interested and prospective customers as well. Additionally, it becomes harder for you to provide content which your customers will actually engage with or even read on your site.

When you bring effective outreach and content together with the brand image, you will find that your SEO becomes more successful in providing the relevant traffic to the site. Moreover, you get the chance to support the branding campaign through the development of content, planning out site pages and targeting keywords which accurately correlate to the objectives of the brand.

Once your brand becomes strong enough, you can enjoy certain benefits. For example, your corporate news will be readily shared by the news outlets and your users will describe their experiences. Your promotions will be disseminated by a greater number of people. All of these factors result in an increase in mentions and links, most of which occur naturally.

Trust

There are other benefits to having a strong brand. For example, it will increase the search visibility of your site. Generally, brands that are famous among consumers tend to have a significantly higher conversion rate from paid and organic search. This is mainly due to the trust placed in the site even by a new visitor. As a result, an improvement of brand awareness becomes a competitive advantage. A site that has been optimized perfectly can make use of this advantage to increase its conversion rates further.

User Journey and the Site

The improvement of user journey can be fraught with complications since there is no single or specific way for optimizing a site. Little things such as the payment process can be improved upon. However, the fact remains that the method of purchase is entirely dependent on the users themselves. Factors such as who the users are, what the products are and how much trust they have in the brand affect the payment process for example.

The expectations of the user with respect to the brand and the site need to be understood. This way, the site becomes more effective at converting visitors into paying customers. A famous brand will find that the user journey is a lot more straightforward. On the other hand, a less-famous brand may find it necessary to provide more detail so as to encourage trust and assure the user to continue on the journey.

It is just as important to design the site in such a way that it meets the expectations of the user. This will ensure that they remain on the site. More importantly, you can only achieve this when you combine site design and brand image together in an effective way.

To get a better understanding of this concept, you do not need to look any further than online newspapers. Simply take a look at the broadsheets and the tabloids, and you will understand how site design is employed to garner user trust. You will find that broadsheets and other serious newspapers have their websites designed with a greater degree of clarity. The main focus is always on the text. On the other hand, tabloids will make use of more images. The headlines will be short and crisp. This is done to encourage users to click on the links.

Branding and SEO

When you are building your brand, you need something that can provide the focus for the digital marketing aspect. A strong strategy for SEO can be that thing. After all, it helps you discover the right audience and in producing the correct content for them as well. Top notch SEO can be the final step that allows you to make the most of all visitors arriving at your site. It can help you get the best possible returns on all the investments you made as well.

Building Brand Image with SEO

SEO campaigns tend to include a branded component frequently. Such campaigns involve targeting branded keywords. For example, 'ABC screwdriver' can be a branded keyword in which ABC is the name of the brand. The usage of these keywords allows people are searching in Google for these to see the links of the company at the top of the results pages. Branded campaigns are excellent in SEO as they are capable of attracting traffic that is most relevant to the brand. As a result, this generates the maximum percentage of conversions or leads. At the same time, the overall effectiveness of the SEO campaign is improved because of its high relevance to the keywords being used.

Branded SEO campaigns are good news for branding efforts as well. After all, branded searches enjoy prominent organic visibility, and that provides extra credibility to the brand. Just think about it. Your user searches for your brand but is unable to see your company. What is the user going to think about your company now? There is another reason. As your brand is prominent, it will be impossible for your competition from stealing the show. They will not be able to encroach upon the leads, sales, and traffic that you are generating. In short, branded SEO campaigns not only enhance your brand, but they also protect it.

One of the main components of nearly all SEO campaigns will be the placement of the offsite content on the relevant blogs and sites. From the viewpoint of SEO, offsite content can provide invaluable inbound links to the site. This boosts the organic visibility by a significant margin.

When it comes to branding, campaigns revolving around offsite content will be a great idea. To create effective content for SEO, you must make sure that it is useful, authoritative, relevant and engaging. In other words, you need content which can raise the value of your brand. Offsite content is capable of bringing the brand to new audiences that are willing to share the content on their social media. This way, your brand reaches out to more potential customers. Consistency and collaboration in the production of textual content will be vital for branding and SEO purposes.

Many people make the mistake of considering that branding and SEO are two separate activities. However, the fact is that they can work together in a cohesive manner so that they reinforce each other. This way, both branding, and SEO will be more impactful. It will last for a long time apart from being targeted and measurable. Keep this in mind, and you will find that getting people to recognize your brand becomes an easier task.

Chapter 12: Emotions and Building a Brand

In your day to day life, you may have noticed that it is quite difficult to fight against the feelings of people towards anything. It is more difficult to bring about a change in their feelings. Well, this is applicable to brands as well.

You see, the emotional involvement of a consumer in a brand tends to increase as he or she experiences it over time. The emotional connection will grow depending on whether the products and services offered by the brand are good or not. If the expectations of the consumer are met or exceeded, the emotional connection will become stronger.

The creation of this emotional involvement starts with the development of a good service or product. The product or service should deliver the value that the customers demand or meet their needs. It is not possible for the brand to grow if nobody wants to purchase the services or products that it offers.

Consider Facebook. Now, this brand is continuing to grow in spite of the fact that there have been several serious privacy concerns from the user. Why is this happening? Well, the fact is that Facebook is pretty useful. Moreover, it allows people to connect with one another. As such, it is an emotional brand by its very nature. Therefore, users are willing to accept the lack of privacy simply because they are able to use the product which is useful for them.

Another excellent example of emotional involvement in a brand being beneficial is Toyota. There have been a few high-profile recalls by the automotive brand in recent years. One of those recalls was instigated after product failures. In spite of these issues, consumers remained loyal to the brand and kept buying Toyota cars and even advocate their usage. This was mainly due to the high degree of emotional connection that the consumers had to the reliable products that Toyota had been offering for years. As such, recalls and failures were not enough to ruin the trust that the consumers placed in the company. The consumers kept faith with the brand and its ability to make things right.

These are just a couple of examples that highlight the impact of emotional involvement in branding. Emotional involvement can result in a cult status for the brand and improvement of brand advocacy. Ultimately, it can result in the creation of a relationship brand, something all brands strive for. As such, it is vital for you to figure out how you can develop an emotional connection between the customers and your brand. Follow this up by cultivating that involvement.

Emotional Triggers and Brand Messaging

You have already seen the importance of brand emotion in the above lines. As such, it is time to start learning how you can appeal to the emotions of the customers through your brand messages and experiences for building the brand emotion. After all, you shouldn't be expecting your customers to become emotionally involved in your brand just like that. You need to deliver messages and experiences which can help them in forming their own perceptions about the brand.

To do this, you need to appeal to the emotions of the customers through your brand messages. In fact, doing so is an integral component of the development of brand messages. It does not matter what copy or content you are writing; the messages should always craft with the usage of emotional triggers.

If you want to drive your customers into action, you must appeal to emotional triggers. In fact, this is the most effective and powerful ways of doing so. If you have seen the messages used by non-profit organizations, you will understand why this is the case. Their messages are heavily charged with emotions so that they can boost the donations they receive. Their messages are successful in all aspects simply because they appeal to the emotional triggers of guilt and compassion in the viewer.

Now, the range of emotional triggers which can be used for crafting your marketing messages is pretty extensive. Some of the most common emotions used in branding are given below.

Guilt: Guilt can be a pretty powerful emotional trigger. While often used by NGOs, this emotion is often targeted by other brands. Travel and tourism brands, for example, can use guilt to target busy parents who are unable to spend enough time with their children.

Fear: There is no one who enjoys feeling that they will be left behind or will be vulnerable. Fear can be a powerful emotional trigger and is often used by insurance brands for their life insurance and retirement savings plans. Home security companies also tend to use this trigger. These companies are rather good at using this emotion as you may have noticed.

The Wish To Be Cool: Lots of people want to come across as being cool and hip. They want to be seen as trendy and fashionable. This emotional trigger is, therefore, quite a popular choice and is employed by a wide range of brands operating in various markets, from lifestyle to fashion to home improvement.

The Wish to Belong: Apart from being cool, most people desire to belong to a group. As a result, this is another popular emotional trigger. Brands craft messages that inform that the customer can become a part of the group or family that they want resulting in a perception of inclusion.

As the familiarity of the customers with a brand begins to increase, they will start experiencing emotions towards the said brand. If the emotions are of a positive nature, they can result in brand loyalty. That, of course, is the ultimate aim for any brand.

It is not just brand messages that should be evoking emotions. The brand experiences should do too. Whenever a customer experiences your brand, he or she should be feeling a set of emotions that is consistent.

A perfect example for this would be Disney. Whenever you experience anything with the Disney name on it, whether it is a movie or a theme park, you will have a certain set of emotions associated with that experience. Those emotions will be related to fun, childhood, family and joy among others. Now, that set of emotions will always be consistent across all experiences. Fans of this brand love the fact they are able to enjoy the same emotions consistently no matter which product or service of Disney they are going for.

In other words, branded experiences include any and all interactions a consumer will have with the brand. It might be something as simple as visiting the site or visiting the store. It may also be looking at the ads or actually using the brand. Irrespective of the actual activity, the emotions experienced by the customers should be consistent with your brand promise.

Brand Loyalty and Emotional Branding

People tend to have a degree of loyalty towards anything that they have an emotional connection to. This is basic human nature. Interestingly, this extends to brands as well. When it comes to the generation of emotional involvement in the brand, there are mainly three steps that you need to follow. They are outlined as follows.

In the first step, your brand will have to deliver a consistent message so as to make your customers become involved in the brand emotionally. In other words, it is all about consistency.

Next, customers will only become involved emotionally in a brand when there is an expectation of that brand being available for a prolonged period of time. At the very least, the period of time should have a predetermined end that has been accepted by all. Therefore, the brand should be persistent and sustainable with its products or services.

Finally, customers tend to become emotionally involved when they get peace of mind from the brand. The customers need to be able to trust the brand in order to feel an emotional connection.

If you keep these points in mind when developing strategies for brand marketing and brand growth, you are certain to attain better results. This is due to the innate desires of people. Consistency, sustainability, and trust are what all people need in their daily lives, and they remain at the top of their minds when choosing brands as well.

When will people become loyal to your brand? Well, they need to have an emotional connection to the brand. They must feel secure that your brand is going to meet their expectations down the line as well. When you ensure these things, the chances of the customer becoming loyal increase greatly. Once that happens, the customers may go out of their way simply to buy from your brand even if they need to overcome little difficulties to do so. At the same time, they are going to be talking about the brand with the other people. Such word of mouth advertising can be pretty powerful and is something that no amount of money can buy.

This can also lead to the development of a cult following. Customers with an emotional connection with the brand may find other people with the same sort of connection. This leads to the creation of a cult and the brand transforms into a cult brand. This means that there is a niche audience that the brand can cater to. At the same time, this niche group is made up of loyalists, and they will be advocating the brand for free. They will even be looking for ways by which they can experience the brand together.

With the growth of the cult brand, a bigger audience made up of loyal customers will be created. With that, the brand grows into what is known as a relationship brand. Relationship brands are the most powerful type of brands. These brands generally fill a specific void in the lives of its customers. Moreover, customers will be looking for ways they can experience the brand in groups. They may even create their own unique ways for experiencing the brand. This leads to the generation of content by users on the web and social media.

Meetups and other events start becoming more popular among the most dedicated and loyal followers of the relationship brand.

Some of the most popular relationship brands are Star Trek and Star Wars. They are perfect examples of how much people can become emotionally invested in a brand. With the continued growth of these brands, their loyal following is expanding as well.

This is how emotions can affect the brand building process. Focusing your efforts on the emotions of your customer can be pretty helpful in building a strong brand. In the next chapter, we shall be taking a look at another important part of branding, the logo.

Chapter 13: The Logo and Its Effects on the Brand

It is not uncommon for people to mistake branding and the logo of business as one and the same thing. The fact is that the logo is just one part of the branding efforts, albeit an important one. The logo is a symbol which can provide the customers with instant recognition of the business as well as the products and services offered but it. It is a powerful method of brand recognition.

Before you start the process of creating a logo, you must be absolutely sure of the brand strategy that you have developed. After all, the logo is not just a pretty picture. It is a small ad for the company. If there is no strategy behind the development of the logo, you may discover that the wrong message is being sent by that logo. In turn, your brand strategy weakens significantly. It is important to ensure the consistency of the brand messages so as to help in enhancing the consumer recognition.

Remember that the aim and the function of the logo are to showcase the goals and the values of the company. As such, these details must be clearly determined before you start designing the logo. Be absolutely clear about the message that your brand should convey. This way, your logo will be able to reflect that message clearly. There must be a powerful connection between the brand and the logo.

The logo must reflect professionalism. It must also signify growth irrespective of the actual size of the company. You should also ensure that the logo is something that can be used in an effective manner year after year. After all, it determines how the consumers are going to recognize the company.

These days, it is extremely difficult to be established in the world of business. After all, a logo is a lot like a mental shortcut to the company or the product. The main power of the logo is due to its visual nature. Various studies have shown that human beings could recognize images and relate to them much faster than they can do with text. Since today, marketing is all about multimedia; this has become rather important.

On the other hand, you should not expect that just about any logo will work for you in the creation of a brand identity. A logo that has been created without much thought can easily and quickly destroy the image of the company. A logo that has been carefully thought out and designed is capable of reaching out to the customers and communicating with them the value of the brand. In short, the bulk of your marketing efforts depends on the logo.

The Logo Creates the Image

These days, the image is everything in the corporate world. The way you are perceived by the customers will have a direct impact on the bottom line. Now, the image is affected by the logo. Take a marketing company for example. Its logo should be a bold one and capable of reflecting aggressiveness. This is a quality that customers will desire in a marketing company. However, an insurance company should have a logo that reflects dependability and solidity. That is the image which customers prefer for an insurance company.

On the other hand, there is no shortage of logos in the world. As such, it is critical for the logo to be meaningful. It should represent something that is unique and specific to the customer subconscious. That way, it will remain unique in the competition.

The Logo and Customer Loyalty

The logo is not just limited to the image and the identity of the brand. One of the reasons why a logo is effective is the repetition. Remember that familiarity is vital to the growth of your business. For brand loyalty to occur, you need a logo with recall value.

Once customer loyalty has been established by the logo, you need to repeat the logo several times. Your logo must accompany all mentions of your company or any service and product wherever possible. This way, customers are going to become familiar with the logo and start relating it to the company. With time, even a part of the logo can remind the customer about the company.

The Power of This Marketing Tool

With careful marketing and time, it is possible for the logo to become the leading factor for sale. Consider Nike. Its logo, the Swoosh, has become one of the most recognizable symbols in the world. The company has run successful marketing campaigns that present its brand as the maker of the best quality sports gear in the world. Now, when presented with two identical pairs of sports shoes with the only difference being the presence of the Nike logo in one pair, a customer will always opt for the Nike pair. That is the power of a logo.

The Logo and Ownership

The logo is a lot like the signature of the company. Since it is a legally recognized part of the company identity, the logo can provide proof of the legal ownership of the company. As such, it can act as a safeguard against forgeries and fakes. Many unscrupulous businessmen create forgeries with the logo of brands to increase their sales. However, it is possible to sue those companies whenever your logo is being reproduced without your permission.

At their most fundamental level, a logo is created for the purpose of identification. Logos do so by the use of icons, marks, symbols, text or images. These days, there are an incredible number of logos out there. Everywhere you look, you can end up finding a few logos. Now, some of them are amazing while others are less so. This gives rise to the question as to what makes a logo stand out and be effective for the company it represents.

As such, it is a good idea to look at the qualities which can make a logo be an effective one.

Simplicity

When designing a logo, make sure that it is simple. Never overcomplicate matters. After all, you will want the logo to be recognized easily. For that, it has to be simple. This way, the logo becomes a quick way for the customers to notice and recall the brand. Complicated logos prove to be difficult to maintain and reproduce. At the same time, they are unable to engage the audience effectively.

You should think of the logo as an elevator pitch for potential customers and clients. For an elevator pitch, you will never have the time to talk about your business in its entirety. Summarily, the logo should not be detailed.

So, how do you do it? Simply get someone to describe the logo. People should be able to take one single, short look at the logo and describe it crisply. They should not take a lot of time simply to get a sense of what the logo is.

Distinctive

As mentioned earlier, there is now an incredible range of logos in the marketplace. Therefore, it has become rather challenging to start apart from the competition. Nonetheless, you need to make sure that you are different from the rest if you want to capture the attention of the customer base. If the logo design is not distinct, it will become harder for the potential customers to recognize your brand. Even worse, they may end up mistaking your company with that of a competitor. As such, they may end up going to the competition instead of choosing your services and products.

When you are selecting your logo, think about how unique it looks. Make sure that it can be easily distinguished from the other brands, especially your competition.

Versatility

Gone are the days when a logo was just printed on a newspaper or shown on the television. The range of mediums has increased radically, making it necessary to have a logo that can work on all of them. If you want your logo to be great, you must ensure that it can be printed in various sizes on different mediums without losing its impact. In other words, the logo should have the desired impact when used on the web, in ads, on video, and on paper among other things.

The logo must look great when printed in black and white apart from color. It should look amazing when printed in small as well as when printed in large sizes. A common technique used by logo designers is to create a black and white logo first before making a colored version. This is the way you should check   your   logo   as   well.

Suitability

When selecting a logo, consider the industry you are in. It must be suitable for the kind of business you operate. However, the logo does not have to be completely obvious. Think about the logo of the famous fast-food chain, McDonald's. Instead of using any symbols related to their business such as burger, they simply chose the first letter of their name and used it to create their iconic logo.

The aim here is to create a logo which communicates the correct tone about your business. It should hint at the type of business you are operating.

Targeted

This goes without saying, but you need to make sure that the design of the logo is suitable for the intended audience. Understanding the audience is one of the primary rules of marketing and branding. As such, always consider the customer when you are designing the logo. The logo must be able to connect with the audience you are targeting. It is not just about the symbol or the text you will be using in the logo.

You need to consider the font and the colors as well. All the elements of the logo should appeal to the intended audience.

Memorable

In order for the logo to have a recall value, it must be memorable. It should leave an impression on the viewers. It might be difficult to ensure this aspect, but it is pivotal to the success of the logo. A great logo is one that a person can recall clearly and even describe it to other people in spite of seeing the logo only once.

Timelessness

It is easy to choose a logo that is trendy. However, all trends fade after a time. You do not want your logo to fade from the memory of the targeted audience after a time. Trends in fashion or lifestyle change with time. However, a logo must be resistant to the change. It should be timeless in its appeal so that it keeps drawing in customers year after year. After all, it is a part of your brand identity. You do not want your identity to change every now and then, do you?

A logo will be the face of your company. It is one of the most crucial aspects of building a brand. Therefore, it will certainly help you out if you spend a lot of time in figuring out the tiny details to get the logo just perfect. Remember that you may not fall in love with the most suitable logo right away. However, remember that the logo is not about you but the brand. It may take the time to grow on you. With the details you found here, it should now be easier for you to find a logo that meets your requirements.

Chapter 14: Simplicity in Brand Building

One of the most underrated aspects of the brand building is simplicity. Just think about it. Some of the most popular brands in the world are also those that help in simplifying the life of customers. These brands cut to the chase and deliver exactly what the consumers want and that too at the moment they want it with very little hassle.

One of the most discussed topics in recent years has been the attempt by marketers to create better experiences for the customers. However, this does lead to a few interesting and essential questions. For example, can increase the time spent by the customer with the brand help in the development of experiences which can increase the engagement of the customers with the brand? Looking at it from the perspective of the customers, will the customer-brand experience need to be simplified to enable the consumer to spend more time in experiencing life rather than the brand?

The fact is that marketers will have to reconsider the elements that make up an amazing customer experience. The majority of customers want brand engagement that is simpler, faster and more seamless. After all, time is limited. As a brand, you need to ensure that your customers feel that their time is being valued.

All of these points have been clearly underlined by the Global Brand Simplicity Index. This is a study conducted annually by Siegel Gate. The study aims to understand the impact made by simplicity on the behaviour of the consumers and the performance of the firm. It also studies the brands as well as the industries which create the simplest experiences possible. Finally, it also studies the top brands which are driving disruption with the help of simplicity. The 2017 edition of the study has revealed the following key findings.

- Simplicity helps brands earn a premium: In fact, up to 64% of customers are prepared to pay more to enjoy a simpler experience.
- Complexity can be expensive: Brands which do not provide simple experiences are losing out on an approximate share of $86 billion.
- Simplicity can build loyalty: Up to 61% of customers are more inclined to recommend a brand due to its simplicity.

- Simplicity enhances performance: It has been noticed that a stock portfolio of the global brands that lead in their usage of simplicity will outperform the major indexes by as much as 330%.

- Simplicity can drive disruption: The major brands which are disrupting their industries are able to do so partially because they offer a simpler brand experience to the customers.

- Simplicity can inspire: Up to 62% of the employees working in simple companies tend to be brand champions as compared to 60% of employees working in complex companies.

One of the most interesting things about the study is that half of the top 10 companies are disrupters and start-ups. In fact, the company in the lead is Dollar Shave Club, an organization bent on disrupting the field of men's grooming. So, the question arises as to how these disrupters have been able to deliver simplicity. It is certainly interesting to note how they can deliver excellent customer experiences along with brand experiences. The following sections will throw some light on it.

Empowering the Customers

One of the most important features of disruptors is that they shift the power to the customers from the brands. Consider Airbnb. This organization has taken power previously wielded only by hotels and provided them to the residents of a locality. These residents are now able to rent out their properties which were vacant, be they spare rooms or entire houses. These residents are able to do so without getting bogged with the complex industry protocols.

Reimagining the Brand Experiences

Another thing about disruptors is that they transform customer experiences that were previously boring and underwhelming to something quite enjoyable. In other words, the experience is completely revamped giving customers a reason why they should spend some time with the brand.

Getting Rid Of Bumps

One of the main reasons for the success of the disruptors is that they identify the problem areas in normal processes of everyday life and provide a solution that gets rid of those issues. Consider Uber as an example. It has proved to be of immense help to commuters who are unable to hail taxis. Uber allows these commuters to use their phones to get their own taxis. At the same time, it provides the user with the cost details of each ride even before the pickup arrives. This makes the pricing much clearer to the commuters and is a service that most conventional taxi services do not provide.

Saves a Lot of Time

Finally, the disruptors end up saving the time of customers. They do so by providing their services at the right moment and place to fulfil the needs of the customers. Online stores are a prime example of such a function. They are able to help people save a lot of time in commuting to groceries and malls by enabling them to shop online instead. The items ordered are delivered right to the doorstep of the customers who spend less time traveling, standing in line and returning.

A Foundation of Simplicity

As you should have identified from the above points, simplicity is at the core of the value propositions offered by the disrupters. In fact, the success of these brands can be credited to the fact that the brands provide a solution to an existing problem. More importantly, the solution is the simplest possible, and it prioritizes the customer experience.

This attention to simplicity made a direct impact on their rankings. As mentioned previously, the disrupters claimed 5 of the top 10 spots. This shows that the disrupters are certainly capable of teaching the more established companies a lot about the simplification of their business.

However, everything is not smooth for these companies. Quite a few of them are currently undergoing issues with regulations. Nonetheless, the disrupters understand and know how they can evolve. These companies are challenging the traditional complexity of the industries and creating their own rules for service delivery. They are enhancing consumer expectations by giving simplicity the priority when it comes to customer experience. They offer experiences which are not only clear but also fresh. As such, they are reaping the rewards.

The fact is that growth tends to bring about an increase of complexity in a brand. This may happen overnight or may require a few years. Nonetheless, complexity does happen. Once it does, brands tend to suffer a lot. Most established brands with a degree of complexity know that it is harmful to their brand. They can certainly learn a lot from the disrupters, but most are unsure as to how they can start. The following points can illuminate these brands.

Begin With the Customers

The first step for any brand for achieving simplicity will originate with how it interacts with customers. It must make sure that customers are able to understand the brand and do business with it easily. This is not just about communications but also the products.

You should look at your brand from the perspective of your customers. Find out how the experience is when trying to purchase one of the products you offer. Is it easy to get more information about the products? How easily can you use the products? These three experiences are vital to the customer, and you need to take a look at each of them.

As you have already seen, simplicity can have an impact on brand loyalty, revenue, and other elements. It does not matter what kind of company you are. You must always remember that the customer experience is pivotal. You should always check all the touch points in the user journey.

Enhance Your Mission

You must engage the entirety of your organization. It is vital for everyone to know that simplification is a priority for the company and agrees to it. This way, any barriers that exist between the various groups inside the company can be eliminated. After all, simplification is not something that can be done in isolation.

It can be a challenge to get the various groups inside a company to cooperate, and this poses a major roadblock to simplification. The groups must learn to let go of their competing interests so that they can bring about an effective change in the way the business is being conducted. They must be able to simplify their offerings and experiences while achieving the desired results as quickly as possible.

The fact is that these barriers are certainly real, but they are by no means insurmountable. You need to get your employees engaged with respect to simplification and make them an integral component of the process. Once employees understand the roles they need to play individually in the business, it becomes easier to get rid of the complexities. Cut down your focus to a small number of amazing initiatives with the help of small teams. Clearly, outline the responsibilities of those teams. This way, it is easy to achieve the simplicity.

Check Everything

Ensuring simplicity is an exercise that requires you to take a look at the entirety of the organization in detail. Instead of feeling overwhelmed, start by creating a plan. You must be empathetic but uncompromising and fearless in your approach. It does not matter which business process you are examining; you must make a thorough analysis of all that is absolutely essential and start to peel away the complex layers of everything else.

Remember that simplicity can only be cultivated through empowerment. As a result, it is vital to invite input from all the levels of your organization. In fact, you must actually encourage it.

Clearly, Define the Purpose

You should start with your purpose. Clarify and define it properly. You need to be clear about what it is you do and how you do it. Once everyone becomes clear about it, you will find that everything else becomes a lot simpler. Moreover, a simple purpose is often an incredibly powerful one. A simple purpose can streamline your communications. It can clarify the intent not only internally but also externally. It can help in defining the path you take apart from your products. The aim here is not to forget that purpose.

Creativity

If you want to manage complexity effectively, your leadership must possess creative skills. Bold actions are also a necessity. Do not let anything remain immune from criticism. You should also avoid incremental change. You may feel like making extensions and amendments. However, all of these things generally end up creating more complexity instead of reducing it.

Studies have shown that CEOs consider that creativity is one of the most important skills that leaders can have. In fact, it can even be more important than other leadership attributes. Moreover, a top-notch CEO will never be afraid of re-examining the things that they have created. They will not be afraid of reviewing strategic approaches that supposed to be proven with a critical eye. Therefore, you need to be brave enough to start over again if you want to be simple.

For any company that has tasted success, growth is not only welcome but also unavoidable. On the other hand, complexity usually ends up accompanying growth. As a result, companies need to take steps by which they can simplify the processes while creating clear and fresh brand experiences. To commit to simplicity, change will have to start at the very top of the organization. The senior management must become committed to bringing about changes which can encourage simplicity.

Chapter 15: Building a Brand

Brand building is a vital aspect of business development. It will not only increase the consumer awareness of the brand and its voice but will also provide it with an identity. These days, there are now several interactive and participatory platforms. They have provided businesses the opportunity to enhance their brand awareness and brand equity.

Before you dive into the world of brand building, you must remember that brand building will take up a lot of time and require lots of resources. With that in mind, you can start with the following chapter to learn how you can create and develop a successful brand.

Bringing Together the Brand Team

All successful brand building initiatives start by bringing together the brand team. The leadership of the organization will create the imperatives from which the brands will be developed. However, those imperatives are going to be articulated and put into action by the people of the organization. As such, you will need a team which can help in making the brand a reality. The team should be cross-organizational which means that the members should be drawn from all relevant teams and groups in the organization.

This way, the team will be able to provide invaluable insight to the organization. At the same time, it will become easier to launch as well as maintain the brand because of their initial participation. Choose the team with care as the success of the brand building exercise depends on it.

Analyzing the Business

Next, an analysis of the business must be conducted. The strengths, as well as the weakness of the company, have to be understood. The competition along with the industry must also be analyzed before meaningful solutions can be developed. Of course, this can be difficult for you. After all, it is your company and, therefore, difficult for you to be objective about it. Nonetheless, you must make an effort to do so.

Analyzing the Audience

Branding is ultimately about the customers. The customers will be the ones to decide if the company is a fantastic success or a spectacular failure. A brand is supposed to attract the audience. How can it do that when it does not even know who the audience is supposed to be? Therefore, you must gain an understanding of how you can motivate the audience and use that information to develop the brand accordingly. This is quite important. As such, you must analyze the various details of the audience that you are trying to attract.

Define the Brand

In this phase, you will be determining exactly what your brand stands for. There are quite a few things you must take into account when you are trying to define the brand. You must have already identified the core strengths of the brand that make you stand out. It is important to know what the brand stands for. The brand values must also be clarified. The brand values should showcase that the company contributes in some way to the economic, social and environmental health of the customers.

Developing the Brand Position

Positioning is about the competitive nature of the brand building. You must provide a unique value to the audiences. This way, your company will be able to capture a piece of the market and make it your own. To do so, you must discover the difference between your company and the rest of the organizations in the same market. That, in fact, is the heart of the brand building process.

Positioning is also about the promise your company makes with the audience. You define a unique value you will be providing to the audience. You will then be ensuring that the company consistently delivers on this promise. The ability of your company to follow through with this promise will ultimately make or break the relationship your company shares with the audience.

Developing Visual and Messaging Style

The messaging and the visuals that accompany the brand will play a pivotal part in the brand building process. The verbal, as well as the visual elements which will be communicating the brand position, are going to attract and convince the audience to start and keep engaging with the brand. They are the result of the brand positioning.

Remember logos? Well, they are one of the visual elements. Other visual elements include the colors, shape, typography and the look and feel of the brand in terms of environments and communications. As for the verbal elements, they will include the mission and the vision statements along with the brand positioning statement. The tagline and the brand are also verbal elements.

Launching the Brand

It can be extremely challenging to implement the brand. To make it easier, you must make the process a collaborative one. All the groups and teams in the company must be a participant in the launching process. After all, people are likely to support what they have managed to create. The implementation phase will also require the internal audience be informed about the brand positioning among other things.

Reviewing the Brand

A brand is by no means static. It is certain to go through a number of motions over time. The brand strategies you implement will affect how your brand is going to change. It can grow and strengthen with time or remain the same as before. In some cases, it might even end up receding with time.

There are certain to be new changes, circumstances, and events which can provide you with opportunities as well as challenges for the enhancement of the brand value. In some cases, you may even have to re-establish the brand. All of these things make it necessary to remain in control of the brand building activities.

As the brand name experiences growth, the expectations as well the responsibilities will keep increasing with respect to the brand building. If you want to ensure the growth of the brand, the best way would be to review the activities and examine the success. Don't forget to use metrics for this purpose. Reviewing these aspects on a regular basis will enable you to make use of new opportunities. At the same time, you will be able to remain true to the brand strategy and vision you had outlined. You will also be able to ensure that the brand is growing in the right direction and is still relevant year after year.

Brand building is far from being an activity you need to undertake only once. It is essential to define the brand and differentiate it from it. After launch, it must be reviewed on a regular basis. Clarity in branding strategies is a must apart from knowing how they are going to be implemented. The brand strategies adopted must be capable of adding value to the customers and help them in developing the right impression of the company.

Now, a successful brand does not happen overnight. It takes a lot of consistent effort over a lot of time for a successful brand to develop. Therefore, it can be pretty confusing as to what you need to concentrate on in order to create a brand that can achieve resounding success. To help you out, we are outlining the following tips.

The Visual Aspects

The visual aspects of the brand are simply the way the company appears to the world at large. This is quite important simply because appearances play a major role in determining the first impressions. In fact, the visuals are the first thing which is noticed by the customers about any company. Therefore, a bad first impression can make it harder to attract customers. You may not even get a second chance.

In order to establish a visual style for the brand, you should select two main colors for the representation of the brand. This is the fastest and easiest way to establish the visuals of the brand. Of course, you may be wondering why you should be using two colors. Well, it is simply because two colors are easier to recall than multiple colors. They can make an impression immediately. Moreover, they can be implemented quite easily. Do not forget to take into account color psychology when selecting the colors.

After the overall visuals have been seen by the customers, they will be reading the messages that you have created. Now, these messages will have to be presented in the correct font. The choice of font or typeface can affect the tone which your brand uses to speak to the customer. Casual fonts can present your brand in a contemporary and friendly light. On the other hand, formal fonts show that the brand is conservative and established.

As such, the choice of fonts depends greatly on the image that you are trying to present to your customers. Do you want your customers to perceive you as a friendly and hip company? Maybe you want to be seen as a respectable brand with years of experience in the field? Choose the most suitable font, and you can do so easily.

Visuals such as graphics and images are no longer just a luxury but a necessity. There is only so much that you express through words before it becomes tedious. The use of images provides a break and can provide a lot more information than what a block of text could. Visuals such as these can be effective in communication, and you need to utilize them for building your brand.

You already know how important consistency is in the brand building process. Nowhere is this more apparent than in the visual elements. Keep using the same set of colors and fonts over and over again. Repeating them will cause the customers to associate the visuals with your brand. Anywhere they see similar visuals; they will end up thinking about you which is one of the aims of branding.

The Verbal Aspects

The verbal aspects are the way you are talking about your brand. Remember that whatever you say will count and affect the customer perception about your brand.

It all starts with the name you have chosen for the brand. If you are an established company already, it might not be possible to do anything about it. However, you can certainly work on the business name if you are just starting out. Choose a name that you are able to live with. It should have a high recall value preferably.

On the other hand, it is quite possible that the nature of the business will change with time. In fact, it might change so drastically that the original name becomes unsuitable for it. Therefore, it is better to avoid becoming too specific with the business name. Instead, you should let the tagline communicate the particulars of the business.

You must never overlook the tagline when considering the verbal aspects of the branding. The tagline is simply the short sentence which follows the business name. This short piece of text is typically used to provide extra information about the offerings of the business.

Unfortunately, most companies rarely put the tagline into proper use. There are several ways to create and use the tagline. You can use it to provide the particulars of the business in case your business name is too generic. The tagline can also be used for informing people about the target audience of the company. Another potential use of the tagline is to provide information about the main unique selling point of the company.

You need to put in a lot of thought into the brand promise you are offering. We have already touched on that. However, you may be wondering where you can start using the brand promise. Well, the brand promise is a paragraph of text, but it can be used in quite a few places.

The brand promise can be placed directly on the home page of the business site. You can even use it for introducing your business when you are attending networking events. It can also serve as an excellent explanatory text on the various social media profiles you will be using.

Like with the other aspects of branding, you need to be using these details on a consistent basis so as to impress them into the mind of the customers.

The Marketing Plan

You will surely be taking steps for creating a marketing plan that works to bring your brand to the attention of the customers. Remember that your success can very well depend on what you are doing with your time. A plan is going to help you make the most of the time that you have.

Before you start, you must get to know and understand your ideal customer. No, this is not the same as the audience you are targeting. The ideal customer will be the consumer whom you want to reach out the most with your offerings. The ideal customer will be pivotal to all your marketing efforts as he or she is the person you want as your customer. Moreover, he or she is the person who not only needs but also wants your products or services. More importantly, he or she is willing to pay for those offerings.

However, the ideal customer is not fixed. It can change with time as the priorities of your brand shifts. Therefore, it can be rather confusing at times to understand whom you are trying to attract. You need to undertake a bit of research to create a complete picture of the ideal customer. Once you know what will motivate this hypothetical customer, you can work your marketing and branding plan accordingly.

The marketing focus is another aspect you need to concentrate on. After all, the marketing focus is likely to change every quarter or every year. Therefore, you will continuously have to decide what your main marketing focus is. For this reason, you must spend some time in thinking and plan out what will be the most vital aim of the brand in the coming months. Your main focus might be to increase the profits or to generate more leads for example. Whatever be it, your branding efforts will need to take this into account.

Once your main marketing focus has been determined, you can start planning out smaller goals. These goals should preferably be related to the main focus as in helping you achieving the main focus. An example would be to break up the main goal into milestones to serve as the smaller goals. You must also pay attention to the timeframe of these goals. They should be achievable within the timeframe of the main focus.

Now that the goals have been set, you will know what you need to do. You should list out all the necessary tasks that need to be completed in order for the goals to be achieved. Make sure that you attach deadlines to each of these tasks so that you and your team can get the necessary motivation to start working. Of course, you should be realistic about the deadlines and the tasks. Implement a bit of flexibility as delays may occur at any given point of time because of unexpected reasons.

Start Acting

It does take time and effort to plan out everything that we have discussed so far. It might even be enjoyable and educative. However, this is not the end. In fact, you have not even started. For starting, you must actually put the things you have learned into action. That may seem like a scary prospect, but it is one that you must do. Otherwise, all effort up to this point is going to be in vain.

You may be learning more about the brand building because you feel that you lack the necessary information and details. You may feel that you need to know everything or that you must master a specific task or activity before you can start. The fact is that you do need knowledge. However, the more you learn, the more you will discover that you need to know.

As such, you should stop and take a step back. Review all the things that you do already know. You already know enough to get started with the brand building process. Therefore, you should start doing so. You do not have to know everything to progress. Remember that there are people waiting for the products and services that you are offering. With time, you can start supplementing your knowledge.

Another common fear is that you do not have the perfect plan for building your brand. Guess what? There is no such thing is a perfect plan. A plan may seem perfect but only in retrospect. So, you need to start putting the plan that you have worked upon into action. Later, you can look back and see how good it was.

When it comes to doing something new, the first step is always the most difficult one. It may even be scary. However, you must remember that all amazing and successful brands have been made possible because someone found the courage to take the first step.

Those people must have also experienced moments of fear and uncertainty. After all, they did not know if things would work out. They may even have been afraid of abject failure. However, they did take the step, and they are serving as your inspiration today.

Chapter 16: Bouncing and Brand Building

As you should have realized by now, building a brand is by no means an easy task. There are several things you are going to have to consider such as the logo, the other visuals, the text, the audience, the brand promise and so on and so forth. However, one of the essential components is still trusted. Unless your customers start trusting you, you are not going anywhere. For that, there are several things you can do. However, we shall be taking a look at this from a different perspective. So, the question is, have you ever been on a date?

A Short Guide to Dating

You might be wondering what dating has to do with brand building. Well, bear with me here. You will get to see what I am talking about in a moment. Before we go on, remember that this is just an example. Therefore, all the ladies out there please do not take any offense.

Suppose you are out with your friends at a bar. You generally have a good time when a cute girl at the bar catches your eye. You see that she is there alone and is simply playing with her drink. It is easy to see that she is bored and in search of good company. Like any gallant gentleman, you decide that you should be the one to provide the company she desires.

So, you go up to her. You start conversing and then ask her for a dance. She happily obliges. You have an amazing time dancing with her, and she is certainly enjoying your company as well. After dancing, you ask her to accompany you to the seat. It feels great to converse and engage with her. Things between you two are getting more comfortable.

Then hunger strikes. Well, it is only natural that you are hungry after all that dancing. So, you get her to accompany you to the eating place. The dinner over which you engage with her even more proved to be an excellent choice. She has already started sharing her secrets and embarrassments with you. After all, you are such a great listener.

However, the night is still young. Therefore, there is no reason why you should not go and have a dance again, right? That is exactly what you proceed to do. Sometimes during the dance, you two break off and go back to the bar. You have more drinks with her. There are also times when you simply go and sit together before heading to the dance floor again.

Finally, it is time to leave. You ask her to accompany you, and she happily agrees. You walk back to her place. Before finally taking your leave, you share an amazing kiss. Of course, you may even be allowed to enter her home. Well, whatever be the result of the night, the fact is that you fulfilled your aim of being with the girl.

Bouncing

So, what actually happened during the date? You spent nearly all of it at the bar. Yet, the girl somehow managed to place her trust in you. In fact, she trusted you enough to let you accompany her home. How did you manage to gain her trust without even stepping out of the bar?

This has been made possible because the technique known as bouncing. You see, you were simply bouncing the girl around the bar. You met her at the bar, took her to the dance floor, to the seats, to the restaurant, to the bar again, to the dance floor again and the seats again. As such, you simply bounced from one place to another with her.

By bouncing from one place to another, the girl feels that she has been with you in several places. It does not matter that all of those places were inside the bar. As such, a feeling of trust is created in her mind. That is how you managed to gain her trust without even stepping out of the bar.

How Does It Matter In Brand Building?

This technique of bouncing is something you should certainly take a look at when you are building a brand. After all, it is about trust, and you need your customers to trust you. By implementing the bouncing technique, you can gain the trust of the customers just like the trust of the girl was gained. With trust, your brand building efforts become a lot easier.

So, how do you do it? Well, you certainly cannot take each and every one of your customers on a date. They might not even like going on a date. Of course, that is not the way. For a company wishing to try out the bouncing technique, social media networks will provide the necessary platform. In other words, sites such as Facebook, Twitter and Pinterest will act as the bar in which you are going to use the bouncing technique.

We shall be taking a look as to how you can do it in the following points.

Create Profiles

The first step of the process is to create profiles on all the different social networks that are suitable for your brand. You have already seen the effect of social media on your branding efforts. Well, the good thing is that you can use this technique along with the other tips already mentioned earlier in this book.

In short, you will be creating the profiles in the social media networks. Then, they are going to be optimized with your branding elements so that they can reflect your brand.

Ask Them to Follow

This is the crux of the exercise. In each network, you are going to ask your followers to follow you, not in that network but on the other networks. In other words, you will be asking your follower on Facebook to follow you on Twitter. In Twitter, you can ask your followers to follow you on Pinterest or LinkedIn. In that network, you can request the followers to follow you on another network.

In other words, you are simply asking the existing followers on one network to follow you on the other networks. A customer may be active on three different networks, and now he or she is following you on all of those networks. Therefore, you are always there on all the networks he or she uses.

Remember the importance of recall and repetition? Well, your brand building messages are now getting repeated across all networks for the customers. Therefore, it becomes easier for them to recall your brand. Isn't that the aim of your brand building efforts?

Bouncing can be a rather excellent technique when implemented properly. You will have to figure out which social networks your customers are most active in so that you can make the requests accordingly. After all, a customer is not going to create a new profile in a new social network simply to start following you. By targeting the ones with the highest percentage of your targeted audience, you can ensure that your messages get across and that your brand building efforts start producing excellent results.

Chapter 17: The Traits of Successful Brands

We have already learned a lot about building a brand. However, you might still be wondering as to what it is that makes a brand great or successful. Well, each brand tends to have their formula for success. They have their own unique selling points as well. However, all successful brands tend to share certain traits and characteristics that set them apart from the not-so-successful ones. We will be looking at those traits in this chapter.

The competition faced by businesses in the majority of industries is incredibly fierce. As such, it has become more important than ever to stand out and create an identity and a value proposition that is completely unique by means of strategic branding. In fact, the effective brand building is often the major reason for many companies that enjoy widespread success these days. The following are the characteristics that are common for successful brands.

Knowledge of the Audience

One of the most important characteristics of a successful brand is its understanding of the target audience. A thorough understanding and knowledge of the demographics of the target audience are essential. You must know what the interests of the audience are and how these people communicate.

The majority of companies will have a particular target audience that they want to attract. By understanding the audience, you get the direction you need for the tone as well as the reach of your marketing campaigns. This knowledge will also help you establish the overall identity of your brand. At the same time, it can help in the creation of an organic connection between your company and your audience.

It is impossible to appeal to all customers. This can be an incredibly counterproductive thing to do as it will cause the diluting of the brand. As such, you need the right approach for your brand building activities, and that can provide an understanding of the target market.

The Uniqueness

We have gone over the importance of uniqueness several times, and that is only because of the acute importance it has on brand building. For the establishment of the brand identity, something distinctive is necessary.

Consider some of the famous brands today. Apple has established its global reputation for the innovative products that follow a minimalistic aesthetic. Domino's Pizza is another excellent example. The uniqueness of this company lies in their evergreen guarantee that their pizza will be delivered in just 30 minutes or it will be free.

As you can see, you do not need a revolutionary idea to create an identity in your chosen niche. You just need to have one special thing which can separate you from your competition. In other words, you can work with a single trick as long as that trick is absolutely fantastic. Once you discover what that special thing is, you must start focusing on it in your brand building efforts. With time, it is certain to garner widespread recognition.

The Consistency

Another point we have mentioned several times in the book is that of consistency. You see, customers generally expect that they will get the same quality level in their repeat visit as they did on their first visit. Of course, they will like it if the quality is better, but they must get the same level at the very least.

This is particularly noticeable in the restaurant business in terms of their food quality and service quality.

There are no customers who enjoy dealing with companies which they cannot rely on in terms of consistency. Since there are several competitors in the industry, customers can easily find some other company for their business. In many cases, inconsistency is enough of a reason to make the switch. This simply shows the importance of following a certain standard of quality in terms of offerings. The customer experience must also be consistent.

McDonald's is an excellent example. It does not matter which outlet you visit; you can rest assured that a Big Mac is going to have the same taste. Moreover, you will know that you will get the same experience in all of their outlets. While the layout might differ, basic elements such as colors and décor will remain consistent.

The Need for Passion

You can certainly create a brand without being passionate about it. However, that will always be about the short-term because it is nearly impossible to sustain the brand in the longer run.

To understand why this is the case, you can simply take a look at the people behind some of the most successful brands in the world. Steve Jobs, Bill Gates and others all had a strong passion for their work. This passion made them work harder and deliver great work on a consistent basis. When you are passionate about something, it becomes easier for you to be enthusiastic about it. You can experience genuine joy simply by working on your passion.

It is not just you who can experience passion and enthusiasm about your brand. It is quite common for customers to become similarly passionate about a specific product or service. Their passion results in referrals and word of mouth marketing.

The Exposure

How can people recognize you as a distinctive brand if they do not even see you? Being able to reach out to the target audience via multiple channels plays a major role in helping your brand be recognized as a successful and distinctive one.

Of course, bigger companies do have the advantage when it comes to gaining exposure. After all, their budget for marketing is larger, and they have more connections already. However, you need to remember that they were once small companies. Moreover, this is the age of the Internet. These days, you have a wide range of tools at your disposal such as social media.

With such tools and avenues open to you, it has become easier for smaller companies to establish their own brands. You simply need to know how you can start using these tools for generating a bigger exposure for your brand.

Being Flexible

If you think that the tastes of your target audience are going to remain the same for years, you need to think again. Change is constant, and this is applicable to your target audience. Your customers are certain to desire new things with time. As such, your brand should also be capable of change. It must be able to evolve with time to meet the changing needs of the environment and audience. Instead of fighting change, you should actually be welcoming it. A flexible brand has a higher chance of success after all.

Engaging the Audience

These days, the creation of a successful brand depends on its ability to create marketing strategies that are interactive and engaging. Such strategies can capture the attention of the customers quickly. After all, customers, these days, want to connect with the brands they like. They even want to be a part of the evolution process of the brand. Gone are the days when a brand could use overt selling techniques and enjoy success.

Social media provides the best platform for audience engagement as you may already know. Therefore, you should start paying more attention to the social networks by making more posts and interacting with the followers.

Now that you know the traits that a successful brand tends to possess, you also know what you must do with your brand. Remember that it will take time and effort. You may even stumble a lot. However, you must persevere.

Conclusion

I hope that this edition helped you to understand the true values of a brand and what it all takes to survive in today's world as a brand company. I also hope that you gained substantial understanding on the use of the Internet and how to create your profiles and blogs in order to appear in the Google Search Engine. It is really important today to have a good ranking on Google if you are a brand because people tend to favor the results which are ranked the highest. The book explained how to use your URL to make that happen and how to link your profiles on different platforms.

If you have a good idea or a brand, do not hesitate to let the world know about it. Simply follow the tips and tricks from this book to optimize your chances fro success. Assess your product/service and think of the target audience. Make a research on what platform works best for you and where the potential customers are hiding. Learn to take criticism in a constructive way and use it to make positive changes.

The Internet is great because it is free and you do not have to pay a lot to advertise your great idea or product. Marketing used to be expensive and significant funds had to be raised to promote a brand or product/service, but nowadays those are unnecessary expenses since people rely heavily on the Internet.

What the digital world also introduced is that people search for information they want to know and look for brands and products they need, as opposed to the pre-Internet time, when they were simply presented with information displayed in newspapers or the TV.

If following the advice from this book, everyone is capable of mastering the social media world and advertising their brand successfully on the different platforms with the precondition that the brand has a unique quality which appeals to masses.

www.ingramcontent.com/pod-product-compliance
Lightning Source LLC
Chambersburg PA
CBHW051720170526
45167CB00002B/731

9 781542 909181